WILD LIGHT

CANADA'S ROCKY MOUNTAIN LANDSCAPE

Photography by Paul Gilbert

Text by Kathryn Graham

Wild Light Press

Library and Archives Canada Cataloguing in Publication

Gilbert, Paul
Wild light : Canada's Rocky Mountain landscape / photography by
Paul Gilbert ; text by Kathryn Graham.

ISBN 0-9695737-2-3

1. Rocky Mountains, Canadian (B.C. and Alta.)--Pictorial works.
2. Landscape photography--Rocky Mountains, Canadian (B.C. and Alta.).
3. Gilbert Paul. I. Graham, Kathryn. II. Title.
FC219.G49 2006   779'.36711'092   C2006-900466-8

Printed and bound in Canada
Printed on acid-free paper

First Printing 2006 by:

Wild Light Press
P.O. Box 67150, N.V.P.O., Calgary, Alberta, Canada T2L 2L2

In the soft light of early morning, the Victoria Glacier is reflected in the still waters of Lake Louise, Banff National Park. (frontispiece)

Alpenglow gilds the mountaintops as the Kicking Horse River rushes through the Natural Bridge, Yoho National Park. (pages 2 - 3)

Bathed in the purple glow of twilight, a group of curious mule deer feed in Waterton Lakes National Park. (preceding page)

A colourful parade of orange and red paintbrush, pink fireweed, and white pearly everlasting with the Valley of the Ten Peaks and Consolation Valley in the background, Banff National Park. (right)

CONTENTS

In a miniature forest, a raindrop decorates the exotic bloom of a calypso orchid.
(right)

INTRODUCTION

Canada's Rocky Mountains provide a powerful attraction for people from all over the world who come to see and experience this awesome landscape. What draws them here? Is it the beauty of the region, with its snow-capped peaks and brilliant waters? Is it the opportunity to have an alpine experience, to breathe the high thin air? Perhaps it is the chance to encounter wilderness or to pit oneself against the elements. The reasons are as varied as the visitors, to be sure, but there are common threads shared by these travellers – the desire to live in the moment in this landscape, to see the colours, the textures and the light, to smell the air and feel the wind, to have experiences that provide personal memories and offer insights into the special character of this place.

For Paul and me, the appeal of the Rockies has always lain primarily in their beauty – the light, the spaciousness, the colours, the textures. Over the years, we have been lucky enough to spend a lot of time here, experiencing different seasons, different weather, different delights. We have learned that every year is unique, with all sorts of variations in the weather and the flora, plus the singular events that add distinctive flavour, such as the sighting of a wolverine or a backpacking trip with friends. Combined, these impressions and experiences have provided us with our own appreciation of the special spirit of Canada's Rocky Mountains.

One of our favourite hikes is the trail to Helen Lake in Banff National Park, as it exemplifies many of the quintessential elements of the Canadian Rockies. We hike this trail at least once, and often three or four times, every year. The trailhead is found along the Icefields Parkway about 35 kilometres north of Lake Louise.

We begin by climbing up through the subalpine forest, inhaling the clean air and watching for the tiny bell-like blooms of grouseberry and the textured leaves of corn lily. We are ever mindful of the possible presence of bears, as it is prime grizzly habitat, and at times the area has been closed because a sow and cub have taken up full-time residence. Although unsettling, the actual chance of seeing or encountering bears adds to the appeal of the hike, for it indicates the truly wild nature of the area.

The path is sometimes steep and sometimes gentle as it crosses over a few small streams and climbs into more and more open forest. Soon we are rewarded with views of the valley – Bow Peak, Crowfoot Mountain, Bow Lake and the Crowfoot Glacier. When we arrive on the shoulder of the mountain we have been ascending, we stop to catch our breath and to gaze down the valley, seeing if we can pick out the pyramidic mass of Mount Assiniboine many kilometres to the south.

A quarter moon sets over the Peyto Glacier in a clear evening sky coloured by rich pinks and mauves, Banff National Park. (left)

Then we turn and head into the verdant meadows. The trees are fewer and smaller here, and in mid-summer the wildflower display is often spectacular – a widespread crazy quilt of everything from paintbrush of all hues to yellow columbine, mauve fleabane, magenta wood betony and pale pink valerian. In moist spots, there are often patches of purple elephant head or white mountain marsh marigold.

Beyond the meadows we skirt a large rock slide, looking for the hoary marmots that bask in the sun atop the lichen-covered boulders. We negotiate the stepping stones to cross upper Helen Creek and enter into alpine meadows. Here we hunt for the miniature blooms of yellow paintbrush and blue-bottle gentian as we cover the open tundra leading up to Helen Lake.

We crest a small rise and suddenly the lake is before us, clear, sparkling and amazingly bluish-green. We pause to admire the scene – the brilliant lake set against the stony slopes of Cirque Peak, the fringe of cotton grass along the near shore, a family of ground squirrels peeping at us.

Then we head up to the ridge, finding diminutive rock gardens of pink moss campion and white mountain avens as we ascend. At the top we turn to survey the route we have taken, looking down on sparkling Helen Lake and out across the expansive meadows to the Bow Valley beyond. We feel as if we are standing at the top of the world.

A few steps further over the ridge and we can see into the next valley to the east, discovering two more turquoise lakes and a rocky polychromatic landscape. We pick out the path of the trail as it heads for Dolomite Pass. We find a sheltered spot to eat a snack while contemplating the afternoon clouds drifting above the towering mass of Dolomite Peak. We discuss the option of scrambling to the top of Cirque Peak – a few extra hours of effort that will reward us with amazing views in all directions, of high glaciers and vast icefields, jewel-like lakes, rugged mountains and endless valleys.

When we descend, we retrace our route, moving from the high thin air of the alpine zone to the flower-filled meadows and then the cooler forest. Approaching the trailhead, we thrill to see a crescent moon hanging in the western sky. At the end of the day we are tired and dusty but happy, having had a short but fulfilling journey into the heart of the Rocky Mountain landscape.

And so we continue to spend time in the Canadian Rockies, reliving the highlights of previous seasons and discovering new delights. We foresee no end to our enchantment with this landscape, with its changing seasons and atmospheres, its colourful wildflowers and spectacular vistas, its brilliant waters and untamed beauty. Like many others, we will return again and again, always hoping to discover a little more of the essence of the Rocky Mountains.

– Kathryn Graham

Fresh greens and rocky textures are revealed on a luminous morning at Consolation Lakes, Banff National Park. (right)

Silhouetted by the setting sun, a hiker stretches atop a rocky outcrop.
(above)

A momentary break in the clouds reveals the morning light on Mount Rundle, Banff National Park. (below)

ESSENCE

How to define the essence of the Canadian Rocky Mountains? Is it found in their very rockiness – their stony, durable, ancient composition? Or does it lie in their height and their grandeur, their steep vertical nature? Certainly, but other factors come into play as well: the ice, the snow and the glaciers, the pure streams and turquoise lakes. The wild nature and ruggedness play a role, as do the numerous forms of life to be found – everything from tiny mushrooms and exquisite orchids to extensive lodgepole pine forests, and from diving beetles and western toads to grizzly bears and golden eagles. The crisp air, the shifting winds and the changeable weather add other dimensions. Then there are the colours in the rocks and in the wildflowers, and the various atmospheres created by different light and the changing of the seasons.

The quintessential nature of the Rockies exists in the alchemy of these key elements: the rugged wilderness, the grand scale and the intimate details, the snowy peaks, the colourful waters, the rich flora and fauna, the changing seasons and conditions, the spacious beauty.

A late summer sunset suffuses the landscape with glowing colours at Waterton Lakes National Park. (left)

The reflection of Mount Robson is framed by weathered branches in the still blue waters of Berg Lake,
Mount Robson Provincial Park. (above)

A fiery blaze of red paintbrush contrasts with the icy blue waters of the Vermilion River, Kootenay National Park. (below)

The setting sun illuminates the underside of the clouds to create an incandescent skyscape. (page 20)

Early on an October morning, a light dusting of snow coats the boulders along the shoreline of Lake Louise, Banff National Park. (preceding page)

An elegant group of fireweed make a graceful display beside the crystal clear waters of Bow Lake, Banff National Park. (right)

22

COLOUR

Colour is everywhere in the Rocky Mountains. Look for it in the faces of flowers: yellow columbine, pink pussytoes, blue camas, green bog orchid, rose root. Find it in the butterflies and the birds: pink-edged sulphur, northern blue, rufous hummingbird, lazuli bunting, golden-crowned kinglet. Hear it in the names of places: Red Rock Canyon, Amethyst Lakes, Vermilion Pass, Emerald Lake.

In the Rockies, colour can be seen in all its moods and measures. It can be bold and brassy in the sunny yellow blooms of balsamroot, in a splash of brilliant orange lichen, or in the golden flush of alpenglow. It can be soft and delicate, as the rosy hues of dawn or the creamy plumes of beargrass. It can be intense, like a searing pink blaze of fireweed, or subtle, like the cool blues and violets in winter shadows. It can have warmth, like the reddish slopes of Pyramid Mountain, or be ice-cold, like the frigid blue crevasses of the Crowfoot Glacier. It can be startling, like the vibrant turquoise of mountain lakes, or the sparkling yellow of larch needles against a bright blue autumn sky. It can be pure, like the soft pink petals of a wild rose. It can be kaleidoscopic, as a lively summer meadow bursting with the multi-coloured blossoms of paintbrush, yellow arnica, purple fleabane, pale pink valerian, yellow columbine, magenta wood betony and blue alpine forget-me-nots.

Wherever it is found – in the peaks, the open sky, the brilliant water, the profusion of wildflowers, or the varied forms of wildlife – and whatever the tone – spirited, quiet, fiery, cool, unexpected, or multi-hued – colour touches our experiences and influences our impressions of the Rocky Mountains.

The sheer cliffs of the Rockwall create a backdrop for the summer spectacle of wildflowers – red and pink paintbrush, yellow arnica, pale pink valerian and the fluffy seedheads of western anemone, Kootenay National Park. (left)

Sunlight infuses a western wood lily with a warm glow. (above)

The first rays of daylight touch the peaks above the brilliant blue waters of Peyto Lake, Banff National Park. (right)

The colourful profusion of a subalpine meadow — mauve fleabane, yellow arnica, red paintbrush, pale pink valerian. (above)

An early midsummer morning along the Continental Divide near Rock Isle Lake offers uninterrupted views, Banff National Park. (right)

Two studies in green and white —
the orderly elegance of bunchberry dogwoods
(right) and an aspen forest (left).

A crisp summer morning highlights the breath-taking scenery of Moraine Lake and the Valley of the Ten Peaks, Banff National Park. (right)

Afternoon light accentuates the curving trunk and the warm autumn colours of an aspen. (left)

WATER & ICE

Ask anyone what makes the Rocky Mountains unique, and chances are that water and ice will be at the top of the list. Their pristine beauty is visible everywhere, as is evidence of their powerful presence in the past.

In winter the Rockies are blanketed in elegant white. As spring warms into summer, snow and ice linger at higher elevations, adding a touch of breath-taking purity to the sky-line. Glaciers grace many peaks and high valleys, and along the Continental Divide there are impressive and expansive icefields.

Meltwater creates the cold clear streams and fills the many spectacular rivers and lakes. The unbelievable blues and greens are caused by the way light reflects off rock flour, tiny suspended particles that also contribute to the curious opacity of the water.

As well as adding a special beauty to the landscape, water and ice build, shape and move mountains. They are not only responsible for the past formation of the mountain rock and the striking contours of the different peaks, but also for the future disappearance of the Rockies. Water is often thought of as soft and ice as brittle, but their abilities to move, to expand and contract, and to carry other materials ultimately make them more powerful than rock.

Both aesthetically and geologically, water and ice are essential elements of the Rocky Mountain landscape.

In the alpine world of Lake Oesa, snow and ice linger into July, Yoho National Park. (left)

In a moist meadow beside a mountain stream, a cheery assortment of wildflowers sprouts up – pink monkeyflowers, yellow groundsel, pale pink valerian. (above)

The awe-inspiring cascade of Takakkaw Falls with a brilliant rainbow in the mist at its base, Yoho National Park. (right)

A winter snowstorm coats the forest in frosty white. (left)

*Afternoon light warms the wintery façade of Mount Hector,
Banff National Park. (above)*

A close look at dwarf Canadian primrose reveals raindrops that reflect the tiny blooms and their mountain environment. (above)

The sunny blooms of arnica flourish beside Rowe Creek, contrasting with the red rock, Waterton Lakes National Park. (above)

MOMENT

What is photography but the capturing of moments? Taking photographs appeals to our desire to hold on to the elusive moods and colours, to preserve the snippets of experience that combine to form our impression of a place.

So many of the events that thrill us with their intensity are short-lived: a glimpse of a solitary elk against the evening sky, the fresh scent of evergreen carried on the breeze, the incredible crack of bighorn rams butting heads, a full moon grazing the rugged mountaintops as it sets, rocky peaks bathed in fiery alpenglow.

As travellers, we collect such moments – sensory memories to carry home with us. We relive the seconds spent looking into a deer's eyes before it flicked its tail and bounded away. We recall with pleasure the cool air that tickled our skin as we hiked upward, and the thrill of the expansive views when we arrived at the top.

Some moments are tinged with fear and a heightened sense of vulnerability: a fall on a rocky slope, a too-near burst of lightning, or an encounter with a bear along the trail. Other moments are comic: the gangly gait of a moose as it crosses the road, young ground squirrels racing and tumbling as they play, a close-up look at a spike of elephant head flowers.

Then there are the moments that are more seasonal: the fresh greens of spring against the still snow-covered peaks, the multicoloured extravaganza of a meadow of summer wildflowers in peak bloom, the bittersweet beauty of the autumn golds, the hushed austerity of the landscape blanketed in winter white.

These moments, these brief bits of time in which we connect with, perceive or capture something unique, together define our Rocky Mountain experience.

A pair of hoary marmots play in a springtime meadow. (left)

The symmetrical leaves of corn lily frame a brilliant burst of red paintbrush. (left)

A colourful medley of red paintbrush, yellow arnica, yellow groundsel and pink fireweed makes a vivid display. (above)

The reflection of the Rockwall in the still waters of Floe Lake creates an abstract scene, Kootenay National Park. (left)

A starry pattern is produced by sunlight sparkling off a mountain lake. (above)

A coyote pauses on its travels through a summer meadow. (left)

A delightful discovery for a flower hunter — a lovely group of white mountain lady's slippers in full bloom. (right)

    The rising sun illuminates a fresh assortment of summer wildflowers in a subalpine meadow—
red paintbrush, yellow arnica, mauve fleabane. (above)

    The crystalline quality of a fall day along the Saddleback trail highlights the golden larches and
pure blue sky, Banff National Park. (right)

LIGHT

In the rarefied air of the Rocky Mountains, the light is clear and sharp but constantly changing. Sunrise can bathe the mountains in a rosy glow, while sunset can momentarily set snowy peaks afire. On moist mornings the light is soft and bright, intensifying colours and softening shadows. By noon on a clear day, the light is often strong and direct, such that blue becomes the dominant colour. As the afternoon wears on, the light angles, softens and becomes warmer. Often the landscape reveals rich violets and golds in the lingering twilight.

The ever-changing weather in the Rockies keeps the light in flux as well, offering photographers a shifting palette of possibilities. Different cloud formations filter and modulate sunlight. Different degrees of humidity alter perceptions of colour and distance. Often the best photographic light occurs on the cusp of changing weather: the dramatic shadows and highlights created by an approaching storm, the moment a cloudburst begins to clear and the landscape is saturated with wet colour and liquid brilliance, or the magic that occurs when sunlight streams through a downpour to paint a vivid rainbow across the sky.

The different seasons bring variations in light as well. Spring light is clean, clear and moist. By the time summer has arrived, the light has become sharp and direct. Fall light is more slanted, with a distant warmth. In winter, the light is cool and pastel in the shadows, but bright and sparkly in the sunshine.

The transitory light of the various hours, seasons and weather reveals the many facets of the Rocky Mountains.

The pristine beauty of a winter morning looking south from Herbert Lake to the peaks of Mount Temple and Fairview Mountain, Banff National Park. (left)

As the morning mist clears, a small island in Lake O'Hara appears in the moist light, Yoho National Park. (above)

Sunlight illuminates a spruce forest the morning after a heavy rainstorm.

PHOTOGRAPHY

To be fully alive, the body must move and the mind engage in the task at hand. This is the ethos that lies behind my approach to photographing *Wild Light*.

Mountain photography is a participatory activity where one moves through the landscape in search of that decisive moment when perfect light and form converge. My style is to be constantly on the move, researching then anticipating where conditions are likely to be ideal, and then going back time and time again, until I capture the images I have visualized. The Rocky Mountains are a tapestry of many colours, textures and most importantly, light. Be it a luminous backlit spruce, a turquoise lake or fiery alpenglow on a distant peak, these dynamic moments present both opportunities and challenges to photographers.

Understanding the subtle qualities of light and exposure are key to making expressive images that elevate the ordinary to the extraordinary. It is important to understand that film and digital media respond differently to light than our eyes do, being more limited in their ability to pick up details in shadow areas, especially in high contrast situations.

Photographing the Canadian Rockies can be difficult due to the range of contrast, from brilliant snowy mountaintops to deep dark valleys. Because of this I am often drawn to that time of day I call the "magic hour", just before sunrise or after sunset. I love making photographs during this quiet time of day with my long-time film of choice, Fuji Velvia. It responds well under these conditions, capturing subtle nuances as well as rendering sharp detail and rich colours.

A brilliant rainbow arcs over Vermilion Lakes and Mount Rundle in the aftermath of a summer rainstorm, Banff National Park. (left)

I prefer a straightforward approach to photography, maintaining the integrity of time and place with limited filtration and digital enhancement. On occasion I will employ a polarizing filter to reduce glare or a grey split neutral density filter to control contrast. At all times my goal is to create images that come as close as possible to reproducing the natural colour and detail that I see with my eyes, since this is, in my opinion, the magic of photography – capturing a moment in time.

Due to my style of photography I like to travel as lightweight as possible, especially when exploring more remote backcountry areas. On these trips it is customary for me to pack my trustworthy Canon 35 mm camera, three or four lenses, a half dozen rolls of Fuji Velvia film, and a compact and sturdy Manfrotto tripod. For less arduous hikes I employ a Pentax 6 x 7 medium format camera as well.

In the Valley of the Ten Peaks, a crisp clear mountain stream sparkles on a brilliant summer morning, Banff National Park. (right)

Miniature angels: a cluster of tiny spotted orchids collects spring raindrops. (above)

*The cool waters of Mosquito Creek flow past a colourful display of wildflowers —
pink river beauty, yellow and red paintbrush, yellow hedysarum, white grass-of-parnassus,
Banff National Park. (right)*

Rosehips add a splash of red to the autumn palette of an aspen forest. (left)

A close-up of one paintbrush creates a wash of red in front of another bloom. (above)

A full moon rises from behind the lofty peak of Mount Robson.

Designed by Paul Gilbert and Kathryn Graham
Text edited by Joanne Mitchell, Blue Systems
Special thanks to Vince Lee

Wild Light Press
P.O. Box 67150, N.V.P.O., Calgary, Alberta T2L 2L2

www.paulgilbertphoto.com